W9-BXE-049

JUNE IS A TUNE
THAT JUMPS
ON A STAIR

JUNE IS A TUNE THAT JUMPS ON A STAIR

SARAH WILSON

Simon & Schuster Books for Young Readers

Published by Simon & Schuster
New York · London · Toronto · Sydney · Tokyo · Singapore

SIMON & SCHUSTER BOOKS FOR YOUNG READERS
Simon & Schuster Building, Rockefeller Center,
1230 Avenue of the Americas, New York, New York 10020.
Copyright © 1992 by Sarah Wilson. All rights reserved including the right of reproduction
in whole or in part in any form. SIMON & SCHUSTER BOOKS FOR YOUNG READERS is a
trademark of Simon & Schuster.
Designed by Lucille Chomowicz.
The text of this book is set in 14 point Breughel 55.
The illustrations were done in watercolor and pencil.
Manufactured in the United States of America   10   9   8   7   6   5   4   3   2   1

Library of Congress Cataloging-in-Publication Data
Wilson, Sarah. June is a tune that jumps on a stair / by Sarah Wilson. Summary: Verses on
rain, snails, the beach, bed, animals, toys, family, and other parts of a child's world.
1. Children's poetry, American.   [1. American poetry.]   I. Title.   PS3573.I472J8   1992
811'.54—dc20   91-4053
ISBN 0-671-73919-0

For Elizabeth Ann, with love

June is a tune
that jumps on a stair.

June is a rose
in a little girl's hair.

June is a bumble
of one small bee.

June is a hug
from the sunshine
to me.

Tick-a-tock
morning,
tick-a-tock
day

both socks on
now,
I can play

sun's in the kitchen,
cat's back
to stay

tick-a-tock
morning,
tick-a-tock
day

Little boats
like paper cups
sailing on a painted sea,
someday when
I'm all grown up,
will you come to shore
for me?

A ride
on Uncle Andrew's
shoulder
makes me bigger,
taller, bolder.
Put together
half-and-half,
we're both as tall
as a giraffe!

A chair
is a lap that's
always flat.

A bed
is a hug
for a small
sleepy cat.

A closet's
a suitcase
that holds all
my clothes.

A curtain's
a tickle
of wind
on my nose.

Wait for me
and I'll be there
and we'll walk home together,
if it's raining
puddle pails
or if it's sunny weather.

Wait for me
and I'll be there
and we'll walk home together.
You wear red
and I'll wear blue,
and we'll be friends forever.

When I stand up
against the door,
I'm taller
than I was
before.

Here's my mark
at two,
then three;
and here I am,
a stretched-up me!

A van goes by
with windows wide.
WOOFA! WOOFA!
Dogs inside!

Woofa-van
with squealy
gears.
WOOFA! WOOFA!
Hold both ears!

My cousin Teddy
wears earmuffs to bed
to keep the ideas
safe in his head.

He says they'll fall out
if the earmuffs are gone,
and then he'll lie thinking
from midnight to dawn.

WHY DID THE CAT
RUN AFTER THE
MUSTARD?

TO CATCHUP!
HA HA HA HA HA

I have a computer.
His name is Ed.
He talks all night
beside my bed.

He prints out jokes
in early dawn
then falls asleep
with his screen still on.

Here it comes,
a toothpaste wiggle,
over my toothbrush,
squiggle, squiggle.
Mushing up
each little bristle,
licky, sticky,
toothpaste wiggle.

Snails unwind a little song
of sunny days
as they glide along
like tiny
boats
on a sidewalk sea
out in the morning
to welcome
me.

Snow-sprung waters,
spangled fishes,
what a friendly wood-stream
this is!

My room's an igloo.
I'm a bear.
Come inside?
DON'T YOU DARE!

Out in the hills
where the wild hawks ride,
a bear cub stirs
by his mother's side
and waits for the sails
of the wind to rise
so he can dance
with the butterflies,
dance with the field grass,
dance with a cloud,
dance with a grasshopper,
laugh out loud.

It's a day for a cone,
for a plum
or a peach,
a warm-spoony day
for a run
on the beach,
where a ball
hits the clouds,
where the sky tips
the sea,
where we jump
for the water,
one, two, *three*!

In and out
the back door. SLAM!
In and out
again. BAM! BAM!

In and out
all through the day.
In for hugs
and out to play.

Good-bye.
Good-bye.
Hello.
Hello.
Do you miss me
when I go?

Screen door's banging.
Click-clack WHACK!
Aren't you glad
that I came back?

We're squirrels in the pathways,
in the brush, too;
squirrels on the rooftops
looking at YOU.

Do you have any popcorn?
Peanuts? A cracker?
Toast in your pocket
or some other snacker?

If you won't feed us,
then count on a row
of squirrels in your footsteps
wherever you go.

The moon slid down
from the nighttime sky
and swam in a lake.
I don't know why.

It climbed in the back
of my old canoe
and turned the lake
into silky blue.

The lilies bloomed,
the fish swam near.
The frogs sang out
for all to hear.

And we sang, too,
for the nighttime sky
in the old canoe:
the moon and I.

A girl
and her flute
needed some light,

so they rolled out the moon
on a summer night

and played a tune so
light and so free

that little notes danced
like silver
to sea.

Gentle waters
rivers
rushes
gentle hushes
from
the
sea

gentle fingers
whispers
touches
gentle you

with me
with me

Little stars
like fireflies
twinkle
through branches
laced in sky.

Amy, our baby,
is wearing new clothes.
She looks like a tiger
all dressed up in bows.
Her face is bright red
when she mumbles
or snuffles.
Do *all* babies
look like tigers
in ruffles?

Grace has tinsel on her teeth
and so does little Artie.
Both of their mouths
are all dressed up
and ready for a party.

My goldfish and I
play a little game.
Whenever he sees me,
he bubbles my name!

A spinning top
is hard to stop.

Whirl-around,
whirl-around,
pop-pop-pop.

But when it's ready,
it will drop.

Bobbledy,
wobbledy,
flip-flap-FLOP!

A spider's face
is hard to find.
If you don't find it,
never mind.

He may not want
to show his teeth
or all his fuzzy chins
beneath.

The rabbit-in-the-moon
has a smile on his face,
watering lettuce
far up in space.

My yellow string beans
are submarines
in a gravy navy
on spinach greens.
I sail them safely
through the straits
of mashed potatoes
on my plate.

Tomatoes fall
like rubber balls,
plip-plop
drop
and
POP!
POP!
POP!

Pull down the dark
when the day is done.
Push it back up
for the morning sun.